GOD

in Three Persons

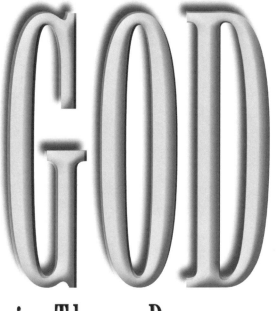

in Three Persons

Biblical Testimony to the TRINITY

Allen Vander Pol

PUBLISHING

P.O. BOX 817 • PHILLIPSBURG • NEW JERSEY 08865-0817

Page design by Tobias Design
Typesetting by Michelle Feaster

Printed in the United States of America

Library of Congress Cataloging-in-Publication Data

Vander Pol, Allen.
    God in three persons : biblical testimony to the Trinity /
Allen Vander Pol.
        p. cm.
    Includes bibliographical references and index.
    ISBN 0-87552-463-X (pbk.)
    1. Trinity—Biblical teaching. I. Title.

BT111.2. V36 2001
231'.044'09015—dc21

                            2001032117

CONTENTS

ACKNOWLEDGMENTS

I express my profound appreciation to the following people, who assisted me in making this work far better than it would have been if I had not relied on them:

The staff at P&R, who showed interest in this project and assisted me along the way.

Rev. Randy Lovelace, who encouraged me to complete this project and assured me that it would help pastors and churches in their ministry of the Word.

Dick and Marian Glazebrook, who advised me concerning how to write for those who are skeptical about the Trinity and gave much of their time to help ensure that my choice of words would not stand in the way of God's Word.

Marcia, my loving and devoted wife, who gives thoughtful editorial advice regarding much of what I write and encourages me in all my work—especially when I attempt to serve the Lord Jesus in ways that are new for me.

May the triune God be honored by this humble attempt to present who the Bible says he is.

INTRODUCTION

As its title conveys, this book is about the Trinity. As you may know, "Trinity" is a word that combines two numbers—three and one—into one word. Admittedly, the word "Trinity" is not found in the Bible, but it is the term we give to one of the Bible's foundational teachings concerning God: that he is three and one. If we know what the Bible teaches about the Trinity, we will possess one of the vitally important truths that we need to know God.

This book has been written to help readers embrace this fundamental truth rather than simply settle for vague notions concerning what God might be like. These notions may come from our own thoughts or from popular opinions about God. In the uncertainty and chaos that result, it can scarcely be said that we know God. A sure framework is essential for our knowledge of God. This book was written to help readers discover who the Bible says God is.

But this book is also meant to fulfill certain specific needs in our quest to know God. First, it is written for those investigating the Christian religion and those who are new Christians—those wishing to learn the basics of the Christian faith. Second, it is written for those Christian believers who contemplate becoming professing members of a church or Christian congregation; as they learn about the church, they need to understand the basic truths, including the Trinity, which the church teaches. Third, it is written for those who have followed a religion that denies the doctrine of the Trinity and who need a forthright guide from the Bible to be assured that the Trinity is indeed a biblical reality.

Yet, all who wish to know God need to know the teaching of the Trinity. Some who read this book may have been professing Christians for many years; others may be investigating the Christian religion for the first time. Whether young or old, advanced in theological training or new to the teachings of the Bible, we all would do well to grasp the truths found in this book. This is so, not because this book presents newly discovered ideas that promise to replace all that has ever been said about God. Rather, the teaching found here is helpful because it states what the Christian church has known about God since its beginning and what God has revealed about himself since the establishment of the world.

We cannot overemphasize how important it is to believe the Bible's teaching concerning the Trinity. This is not a topic for us to consider only when we have spare time. Whether or not we believe this teaching determines whether or not we know the true God. It determines whether or not we are praying to the true God. It determines whether or not we have found the way to be saved by God. False ideas about God are like wrong addresses, which only ensure that the letter will not get to the intended reader. We must know what God is like in order to reach him.

Furthermore, this topic is urgent to know because of how God responds to those who misrepresent him. God has said, "I, the LORD your God, am a jealous God" (Exodus 20:5). God continued by explaining how he severely punishes those who hate him and show it by misrepresenting him. If someone misspells your name or mispronounces it, this may hurt you because others have not been thoughtful enough to learn how to address you. God is "jealous" and is protective of his name. He wants to be understood correctly and addressed appropriately. If we disregard what the Bible says about God and decide to talk about him as we simply choose, we are inviting his punishment on ourselves. Surely, we should want to know basic truths about God so that we can communicate with him!

To examine the crucial teaching of the Trinity we will study the Bible. We will begin with Jesus Christ, the one through whom God revealed himself most concretely; we will investigate who the Bible says he is and what he came to do. Next, we will study what the Bible says about the Father of Jesus Christ and how the Father is associated with Jesus. Third, we will ascertain what the Bible teaches about the Holy Spirit and how he relates to the Father and the Son. Fourth, we will bring together in summary form the biblical teaching found in chapters 1 through 3. Fifth, we will examine a few Scripture passages where all three persons of the Trinity are mentioned side by side; we will observe how they illustrate what has been said so far. Finally, we will seek to answer questions raised by those who deny this crucial biblical teaching of the Trinity.

Perhaps advice should be given concerning how to read this book. Although it is brief, readers should take time to comprehend each chapter before they go on to the next. Also, those who prefer to read a different Bible translation from the one used here are encouraged to consult the translation of their choice whenever the Bible is cited. Any Bible translation that is faithful to the original languages will present the same teaching about God that is found here.

I hope that this book will be used by the Father, Son, and Holy Spirit to assist all readers in knowing him.

Questions

For Review

1. What is wrong with worshiping God according to the ideas we want to have about him?
2. Why is it necessary to know and understand the Bible's teaching about the Trinity?
3. What did God mean when he called himself a "jealous" God?

For Further Thought

4. What do the following verses teach us about God's desire for us?
   a. Jeremiah 9:23–24
   b. Jeremiah 24:7
   c. Psalm 36:10
5. If the Bible presents the teaching of the Trinity, how should we regard religious groups and their "holy books" that deny this teaching? Explain your answer.

CHAPTER 1

JESUS CHRIST, THE SON OF GOD

Let us begin with the one who is often called "the second person of the Trinity."

Centuries before Jesus was born in Bethlehem, the prophet Isaiah predicted the birth of the Savior in a startling way. Isaiah wrote,

> For to us a child is born,
>   to us a son is given,
>   and the government will be on his shoulders.
> And he will be called
>   Wonderful Counselor, Mighty God,
>   Everlasting Father, Prince of Peace. (Isaiah 9:6)

This is startling because Isaiah presents what seems to be a paradox. He writes about a child who is born, a son; this means the child is human. He also says that this son will be "God" and "everlasting." Is it possible that a human child who is born could be the Mighty God, the Everlasting Father?

This puzzle introduces us to the person Jesus Christ. He is the everlasting God, and he was born a man.

He Is Everlasting God

The gospel of John teaches us who this Jesus Christ is. It begins by introducing Jesus Christ as the everlasting God. Using the first words of Genesis 1 in the preface to his gospel, John tells us who was there "in the beginning" when God created the heavens and the earth. John says, "In the beginning was the Word, and the Word was with God, and the Word was God" (John 1:1). A little later the gospel of John says that this Word is the person Jesus Christ. Jesus Christ was there in the beginning of the universe. He was with God, and he was God.

Jesus Christ's divinity (the truth that he is God) can be seen in the fact that he was involved in the creation of the world. John says, "Through him *all* things were made; without him nothing was made that has been made" (John 1:3). This rules out the idea, held by some, that Jesus was the first creature of God and that he assisted God in creating everything else. In fact, "without him nothing was made that has been made." As Exodus 20:11 says that in six days God the Lord "made the heavens and the earth, the sea and *all* that is in them," so John teaches that *all* things were made through Jesus Christ, who is the Lord God.

This evidence of Jesus' divinity is declared in other passages of the Bible as well. From the book of Colossians we learn that "by him all things were created: things in heaven and on earth, visible and invisible, whether thrones or powers or rulers or authorities; *all things were created* by him and for him. He is before all things, and in him all things hold together" (Colossians 1:16–17). When God created the universe, his agent who accomplished the miracle of creation was the divine person Jesus Christ, whom Romans 9:5 calls "God over all."

He Was Born

John continues his introductory story of the Word who was with God and who was God: "And the Word became flesh and made his dwelling among us" (John 1:14). This refers to the time when the "Mighty God" was born to us (Isaiah 9:6). The eternal divine person Jesus Christ, who possessed all the aspects of the divine nature, added to himself our human nature.

The book of Hebrews also teaches about the full humanity of Jesus Christ. It says, "For we do not have a high priest who is unable to sympathize with our weaknesses, but we have one who has been tempted in every way, just as we are—yet was without sin" (Hebrews 4:15). We do not normally think of God as being tempted, yet the Bible teaches that when the divine Word became flesh, he joined us in our vulnerabilities and weakness. He experienced firsthand what it is like to be hungry and tempted. Still, even in his weakness, he never surrendered to temptation by sinning. He remained fully human, yet fully obedient to Scriptures. Jesus is the only human being who has kept himself perfect.

Hebrews affirms further that the human nature that Jesus took on himself was the same human nature that we have. "Since the children have flesh and blood, he too shared in their humanity so that by his death he might destroy him who holds the power of death—that is, the devil" (Hebrews 2:14).

All this is vitally important for us. The Bible says that we are sinners who have disobeyed God's commands. The only way for us to escape the eternal punishment of God, which our sins deserve, is to have someone who was completely sinless and human undergo that punishment for us. Therefore, Jesus rescued his people from eternal punishment by becoming like us so that he could die for us. The Word became like us—thoroughly human—so he could take our place.

The humanity of Jesus explains why Jesus, who is eternal God, prayed when he lived on earth. He was tempted in every way as we are; his human nature was vulnerable and weak. Therefore, Jesus as man customarily turned to his heavenly Father to plead on behalf of himself and for the needs of his followers.

Like the divinity of Jesus, the full humanity of Jesus is a central truth in the Christian faith. "Every spirit that acknowledges that Jesus Christ has come in the flesh is from God, but every spirit that does not acknowledge Jesus is not of God" (1 John 4:2–3). As Isaiah promised beforehand that the child to be born would have the name "Mighty God," so the apostle Peter preached after Jesus came that "Jesus of Nazareth was a man" (Acts 2:22).

He Is God and Man

It is possible to misunderstand what has been written here so far. For example, it may appear that when the Word became flesh, he ceased being divine. However, when the Word became flesh, he continued to be God. He did not merely turn into a man. Rather, he added to himself our human nature. Although he remained one divine person, now he possesses two natures—one divine and one human. This truth perplexes our human minds, but it is possible because God did it.

The Bible teaches this clearly when it says, "For in Christ all the fullness of the Deity lives in bodily form" (Colossians 2:9). In the man Jesus Christ the fullness of God was present. Jesus himself also taught this truth when he called God his Father. He said, "My Father is always at his work to this very day, and I, too, am working" (John 5:17). His opponents were infuriated because this claim, that God was his Father, implied that Jesus was equal with God (John 5:18). It was a claim that led the religious leaders of the Jews to decide that Jesus must be killed. Yet, Jesus never told them that they misunderstood him. They understood his claim accurately; the human Jesus was equal with God because he also was God. It was a truth so fundamentally true about him that he was willing to die to uphold it. As the Bible consistently teaches, he was man and God.

This truth is important for us to know when we seek to understand what happened when Jesus died on the cross.

When Jesus died, his death was not death by accident; it was not death due to old age. His death on the cross was due to God's curse on sin. The Bible says, "Cursed is everyone who is hung on a tree" (Galatians 3:13). There were many who watched the crucifixion of Jesus joyfully. They had grown to hate him thoroughly. Yet, in the final analysis, they did not send Jesus to the cross. God the Father did.

So, while he hung on the cross, Jesus called out, "My God, my God, why have you forsaken me?" (Matthew 27:46).

Jesus died on the cross a perfect man, dying in the place of sinful men and women. Untarnished by sin since conception and birth, he was able to die for the sin that has been present in us since we were conceived and born. But also, being God, he was able to endure *all* of God's punishment, and he was able to die for many. Being God, he could do what was necessary to pay for all our sins, to make the forgiveness we need thoroughly complete. Being God, he was great enough to deal with God for us, and being human he was close enough to us to die in our place. The mystery of God's adding to himself our human nature was the very thing we needed to be saved from our sins. He was the Son of God who could endure God's punishment, and he was man who could pay for human sins.

The Bible tells us to trust in Jesus Christ alone to be saved from our sins. We must turn to God and tell him that we are sinners; we have rebelled against him, disobeyed him, and hated him. The Bible also tells us to turn to Jesus believing that he is all we need to have our sins forgiven. When we believe in him, we trust that he has died for us. The Bible promises, "For God so loved the world that he gave his one and only Son, that whoever believes in him shall not perish but have eternal life" (John 3:16).

To be saved from our sins, we needed this perplexing miracle by which eternal God was born.

This solution for our sins raises yet another question: If Jesus is God, who is this "God" who—according to John 3:16—"gave" Jesus, his "one and only Son"? Let us continue with that question in chapter 2.

Questions

For Review

1. What is the amazing truth taught in Isaiah 9:6?
2. How does Christ's involvement in the creation of the world show that he is God?
3. How did Jesus' divinity and humanity equip him to be the Savior?

For Further Thought

4. Read these four questions and then answer each of them:
   a. Was there a time when Jesus Christ was not God?
   b. Was there a time when Jesus Christ was not man?
   c. Will there be a time when Jesus Christ is not God?
   d. Will there be a time when Jesus Christ is not man?
5. According to the following verses, which other persons are qualified to save sinners? Can you explain from this chapter why this is so?
   a. John 14:6
   b. Acts 4:10, 12

CHAPTER 2

THE GOD AND
FATHER OF OUR LORD
JESUS CHRIST

There are many passages in the Bible where God is called our Father. He is called our Father for at least two reasons. The first reason is that God created all things. We find this implied in Luke 3:38, where Adam, the first man, is called "the son of God." Adam came from God and owed his existence to God. In this sense God is like our human parents who gave us life, for God also gave us life. If Adam is a son of God, we may understand that God is Adam's Father. Similarly, God is called "the Father of our spirits" in Hebrews 12:9. James 1:17 says that God, who gives every good and perfect gift, is the "Father of heavenly lights, who does not change like shifting shadows." In these passages and others God is called Father because he is the origin of the universe and the one who takes care of it.

Another reason why God is called Father is that he saves his people from their sins. Isaiah 63:16 says,

> You, O LORD, are our Father,
>   our Redeemer from of old is your name.

Isaiah says this in a prayer to God. He is asking God to forgive the sins of his people and to return to them with tenderness and compassion. Where else could Isaiah go to ask for forgiveness and help? God had been their loving Father. Isaiah calls God "Father" to emphasize the mercy God shows to the people he saves. Therefore, since God is our Father, Isaiah was able to say in a more familiar passage that a name for Jesus Christ would be "Everlasting Father" (Isaiah 9:6). God is Father because he saves.

So Christians may call God "Father" because God is their maker and their savior. God is the source of physical life and of eternal life.

The Father of Jesus Christ

There are many other places in the Bible, however, where "Father" refers to a person distinct from Jesus Christ. Ephesians 1:3 says, "Praise be to the God and Father of our Lord Jesus Christ." This teaches that there is a person, distinct from Jesus Christ, who is his heavenly Father. That Father spoke on the day Jesus was baptized by John the Baptist. As Jesus was baptized, "a voice from heaven said, 'This is my Son, whom I love; with him I am well pleased' " (Matthew 3:17). This heavenly voice spoke again when Jesus was transfigured on a mountain. While Jesus was on the mountain with Moses and Elijah, the voice said, "This is my Son, whom I love; with him I am well pleased. Listen to him!" (Matthew 17:5). This sound was not the voice of Jesus himself, but the voice of his heavenly Father, who is distinct from Jesus. The Bible makes clear, then, that the Father and Jesus Christ the Son are different divine persons.

As the Lord Jesus Christ spoke, especially in the gospel of John, he repeatedly explained his relationship with his Father and showed that the Father was a divine person different from himself. One such instance was his prayer to his Father in John 17. Jesus prayed, "And now, Father, glorify me in your presence with the glory I had with you before the world began" (John 17:5). By making this request to his Father, Jesus demonstrated the truth that he is distinct from the Father; yet in the beginning they both possessed the same divine glory. When he became man, Jesus put aside his heavenly glory for a while, but he anticipated the day when he would receive it again and he and his Father would share the same heavenly glory. Originally they possessed the same glory, yet they were distinct.

Another time when Jesus showed that he and his Father are distinct was when he described those who opposed him. Many of Jesus' contemporaries did not follow him because they did not comprehend who Jesus was. Even when they saw the miracles performed by Jesus, they did not appreciate that they were witnessing the works of God. As a result they opposed Jesus and the claims he made about himself. But they were not opposing Jesus alone. Inadvertently they also opposed his Father. Jesus said, "He who hates me hates my Father as well. If I had not done among them what no one else did, they would not be guilty of sin. But now they have seen these miracles, and yet they have hated both me and my Father" (John 15:23–24). The fact that Jesus referred to "both" shows that he viewed the Father and himself to be distinct. Although both shared the same glory in heaven and deserved the same reputation on earth, they were distinct persons. The Father is the Father *of* Jesus Christ.

The Father Sent the Son

Although the Father and Son both possess eternal deity and share the same glory, they do not resemble each other entirely. In some ways they are unlike one another. We can see this in the unique task each person fulfilled in bringing us salvation.

The gospel of John identifies God the Father as the one who sent Jesus, the Son. In John's gospel and his three letters, this truth is referred to at least forty-four times: the Father sent the Son. Once Jesus said, "When a man believes in me, he does not believe in me only, but in the one who sent me" (John 12:44). This truth is also present in John 3:16: "For God so loved the world that he gave his one and only Son, that whoever believes in him shall not perish but have eternal life." By giving the Son, the Father sent him into the world. John also teaches, "And we have seen and testify that the Father has sent the Son to be the Savior of the world" (1 John 4:14). Part of the Father's identity is that he is the one who sent the Son.

Since Jesus Christ is the one whom the Father sent to be the Savior, we can understand the unique importance Jesus holds for those who want to know God. He is singularly significant in at least the following ways.

First, since the Father sent the Son, the Son is the Father's messenger to us. In his prayer to his Father Jesus said that he revealed the Father's name to his disciples (John 17:6, 26). When he became flesh and lived on earth, Jesus made his heavenly Father known to us (John 1:18). Ephesians 1:9 says that Jesus made known the mystery of God's will. If you have not been able to contact a friend who has lived far away for many years and you learn that your friend has a son living in your city, you will probably try to contact that son to find out how your friend is doing. Similarly, if you want to know the Father, go to the Son whom the Father sent. Being God himself, Jesus is uniquely able to make the Father known to you (John 1:18).

Another aspect of Jesus' uniqueness is the truth that, when Jesus came, he completed the work that the Father gave him to do. The book of Hebrews quotes Jesus as saying, "I have come to do your will, O God" (Hebrews 10:7). Acts tells us that all that happened in Christ's life was planned by his Father (Acts 4:28). Since Jesus perfectly obeyed his Father, who sent him, we are sure that the salvation Jesus offers fully meets the Father's requirements. Jesus did everything that was necessary to remove our sin and reconcile us to the Father.

Furthermore, when the Father sent the Son Jesus to this earth in the form of a man, he gave him the power and authority necessary to accomplish the Father's work. The Father gave Jesus Christ the power to lay down his life and take it up again (John 10:18). Jesus also claimed that the Father gave the Son the right to judge (John 5:22). This shows again that the Father did not merely send the Son as a man to be the Savior; he also prepared Jesus Christ uniquely with all the authority necessary to save sinners completely and to bring human history to a close.

When Jesus was sent by the Father, he came on behalf of the Father to achieve for us and to offer to us salvation from our sins.

Perhaps we should take a moment to note that this relationship between the Father and Son in our salvation raises the curtain for us to see a little more clearly the drama that took place at the creation. When God created the heavens and the earth, he spoke and the world came into being (see Genesis 1). But we have already discovered from the Bible that all things were made through Christ (John 1:3). This is also how the sinner is saved: through Christ. In each case Jesus Christ, the Son, accomplished what the Father had decided should come to pass. The apostle Paul wrote, "Yet for us there is but one God, the Father, from whom all things came and for whom we live; and there is but one Lord, Jesus Christ, through whom all things came and through whom we live" (1 Corinthians 8:6). As the Father saved us through Jesus Christ the Son, so it was the Father who also created us through the Son.

One Faith

The fact that we have mentioned two divine persons may prompt us to ask whether they require us to follow two different religions. Must we worship the Father with one religion and the Son with another religion?

The answer to this question comes from the truth that the Father sent the Son. Our response to Jesus constitutes our response to the Father. In human relationships we demonstrate respect for our friends by treating with respect the gifts they give us. Similarly, faith in Jesus Christ is faith in the Father who sent him. Jesus said, "He who does not honor the Son does not honor the Father, who sent him" (John 5:23). Since Jesus fully obeyed his Father, trusting in Jesus' life and death means that we trust that the Father's provision of salvation is complete. Since the Father sent the Son, our trust in Jesus is trust in the Father's gift.

Faith in the Son is faith in the Father. This is so, also, because we learn about the Father by learning about Jesus. He alone reveals the Father to us. Therefore Jesus said, "Anyone who has seen me has seen the Father" (John 14:9). Since the Father came to us by sending his Son, we go to the Father by going to the Son. As Jesus said, "I am the way and the truth and the life. No one comes to the Father except through me" (John 14:6).

Questions

For Review

1. How does the Bible show that the Father and Son are distinct persons?
2. What are the distinct tasks of the Father and Son while they work together?
3. In what ways is Jesus "singularly significant"?

For Further Thought

4. A monotheist is a person who believes there is only one true God. Do all monotheists believe in the *true* God? Explain. Read James 2:19 and John 14:6.
5. Is it possible for Jesus Christ to obey his Father and yet be equally great as his Father? Are there parallels to this in our human relationships? Read John 17:1–5.
6. How has the Father loved us? Read John 3:16.

CHAPTER 3

THE SPIRIT OF CHRIST

Along with the Father and Son a third person belongs to the Trinity, the Holy Spirit. When the Bible refers to the three persons of God, the Holy Spirit is often mentioned last, but this does not mean that the Spirit is least important. The order probably reflects the fact that the Holy Spirit's task is to honor the Son and Father. There is a hint of this when the Bible calls the Holy Spirit the Spirit of God and the Spirit of Christ (Romans 8:9). Let us learn who this Spirit is.

He Is a Person

Some people claim that the Holy Spirit is not personal. Since the words used in the Bible for "Spirit" mean wind or breath, they say the Spirit of God is only an impersonal force, as the wind is.

When Jesus speaks about the Holy Spirit, however, he talks about the Spirit having personal qualities. For example, Jesus says, "When the Counselor comes, . . . the Spirit of truth . . . , he will testify about me" (John 15:26). If the Spirit were not personal, Jesus would refer to the Spirit as "it," but Jesus calls the Spirit "he" and refers to "him" (see also John 14:17). We see further evidence that the Spirit is a person by noticing what Jesus says the Spirit does. He gives the help of a "Counselor" and testifies about Jesus; he teaches, reminds, convicts the world of guilt, guides, and tells what is yet to come (John 14:26; 16:8, 13–14). Impersonal forces do not give this kind of personal attention.

He Is Divine

The Bible also teaches that the Holy Spirit is divine — he is God, as fully as are the Father and Son. One way this is shown is in how the Bible refers to the Holy Spirit as equal with God. For example, Peter once said to a man named Ananias who had lied to the church, "How is it that Satan has so filled your heart that you have lied to the Holy Spirit . . . ? You have not lied to men but to God" (Acts 5:3–4). According to Peter, lying to the Holy Spirit was lying to God. What Peter said shows that the Holy Spirit is God.

The Spirit's divinity can also be seen in the fact that he performed the work of God. The Bible shows that he was active in creating the universe, as the Father and Son were. Genesis 1, which reports how God created the world, says that "the Spirit of God was hovering over the waters" (Genesis 1:2). Psalm 104:30 says, in agreement,

When you send your Spirit,
    they are created,
    and you renew the face of the earth.

In the beginning the Holy Spirit was there taking part in the divine work of creating the universe.

The Bible teaches the Spirit's full divinity with clarity, especially when it places his name side by side with those of the Father and Son and ascribes equal honor to all three. Consider Paul's final words in his letter of 2 Corinthians: "May the grace of the Lord Jesus Christ, and the love of God, and the fellowship of the Holy Spirit be with you all" (2 Corinthians 13:14). Notice also how Jesus authorized the sacrament of baptism. The church must baptize "in the name of the Father and of the Son and of the Holy Spirit" (Matthew 28:19). We can see that the Bible presents all three persons, including the Holy Spirit, as equal in divinity and honor.

The Work of the Holy Spirit

Although the Holy Spirit is a divine person, distinct from the Father and Son, it does not follow that the Holy Spirit performs work that is all his own. What the Spirit does he is doing in harmony with the Father and Son. Jesus said that he would send the Holy Spirit and that the Spirit goes out from the Father (John 15:26). Just as the Father sent the Son to fulfill the Father's plan, so the Spirit is sent by the Father and Son to take part in their achievements. The Holy Spirit is called the "Spirit of God" and the "Spirit of Christ" (Romans 8:9) because he is united to the Father and Son in being, purpose, and work.

The unique work that the Spirit performs in God's accomplishment of salvation for sinful humankind can be summarized with two basic statements: He enabled Christ to come to us, and he enables us to come to Christ.

1. He Enabled Christ to Come to Us

We see that Christ was enabled to come to us by the Spirit's power in several ways. When the eternal Son of God added to himself our human nature, he was born of the virgin Mary. His conception was miraculous; it was the work that the Holy Spirit performed in Mary. "She was found to be with child through the Holy Spirit" (Matthew 1:18). Jesus entered the world as a man by the Spirit's power.

The Holy Spirit was active again at the beginning of Jesus' public work of preaching, performing miraculous signs, and calling humanity back to God. When Jesus was baptized, the Spirit of God could be seen descending on Jesus like a dove (Matthew 3:16). Immediately afterward, the Bible teaches, Jesus was tested through temptation, and then he preached publicly about the kingdom of God. Jesus performed this work by the power of the Spirit, who descended on him at his baptism.

The Bible also teaches that, after he was crucified and buried, Jesus rose from the dead in the Spirit's power. "If the Spirit of him who raised Jesus from the dead is living in you, he who raised Christ from the dead will also give life to your mortal bodies through his Spirit" (Romans 8:11). Jesus entered this world as man and he offered himself as the sacrifice needed to pay for our sin—all in obedience to his Father and with the Spirit's power.

Forty days after he rose from the dead Jesus ascended to heaven. From that time on Jesus adopted a new way of announcing salvation to lost sinners. Now, instead of being the preacher himself, Jesus would send his apostles into the world to be his witnesses. These witnesses carried the good news of Jesus to ever-expanding circles of the gospel's influence. Even as these witnesses were sent by Jesus, they went into the world in the Spirit's power. When Jesus told his disciples that he was leaving them, he promised that the Spirit would give them power to be his witnesses (Acts 1:8). The Word that they preached and the Scriptures that they wrote were inspired by the Holy Spirit (2 Peter 1:21).

In every way the Spirit's power enabled Christ to come to us. The Spirit's power brought Jesus into this world and empowered Jesus while he was on the earth. The Spirit's power also brought Jesus' witnesses and the gospel of Jesus to each person who has come to faith in Christ.

2. He Enables Us to Come to Christ

The Bible teaches that a Christian's coming to faith in Christ is the result of the Holy Spirit's work in that person's life. Without Christ a person is dead in sin and transgressions (Ephesians 2:1–2). We all need a new birth so that we can know Jesus as he really is. Unless a man is born again, he cannot see the kingdom of God. Unless a man "is born of water and the Spirit," he cannot enter the kingdom of God, Jesus said (John 3:3, 5). The initiative that prompts a person to trust in Christ is the Holy Spirit.

But the Spirit's power is also necessary for a Christian to continue following Christ. It is this Holy Spirit who develops in us the personal qualities of godliness that God wants and that make us resemble Christ. "The fruit of the Spirit is love, joy, peace, patience, kindness, goodness, faithfulness, gentleness and self-control" (Galatians 5:22–23). Similarly, it is the Spirit of Christ who prompts us to pray. Therefore, even when we do not know what to pray for, the Spirit "intercedes for us with groans that words cannot express" (Romans 8:26). By the Spirit we consciously call out to God as our personal Father (Romans 8:15). It is also the Spirit of Christ who makes diverse followers of Christ form one spiritual body (1 Corinthians 12:13). Just as the Holy Spirit raised Jesus from the dead, so the Spirit will raise his followers from the dead. "If the Spirit of him who raised Jesus from the dead is living in you, he who raised Christ from the dead will also give life to your mortal bodies through his Spirit, who lives in you" (Romans 8:11). We learn from this variety of verses from Scripture that to be God-honoring the entire Christian life must be Christ-directed, but also Spirit-enabled.

When we understand that the Spirit enabled Christ to come to us and enables us to come to Christ, it becomes clear that faith in Jesus Christ is faith in the Holy Spirit as well. By trusting in Jesus Christ alone as our hope of forgiveness from our sins, we are trusting that the Spirit adequately empowered Jesus Christ, completely qualified him, and faithfully presented him in the Bible. Faith in Jesus Christ is faith as well in the Father who sent him and in the Spirit who empowered him. The three divine persons work in concert making it possible for the apostle Paul to say that there is one Lord and one faith (Ephesians 4:5).

Questions

For Review
1. How does the Bible show that the Holy Spirit is a person?
2. How does the Bible show that the Holy Spirit is God?

3. What has the Holy Spirit done to enable Christ to come to us?

4. What has the Holy Spirit done to enable sinners to come to Christ?

For Further Thought

5. What difference does the fact that the Holy Spirit is a person make to the Christian? Read John 16:8, 13–14.

6. If the Holy Spirit were not God, how would that affect the confidence of a person who believes in Jesus Christ? Read John 15:26 and 1 Corinthians 12:3.

7. If a "spiritual person" is a person under the influence of the Holy Spirit, is it possible for a "spiritual person" not to follow Jesus Christ? Explain.

CHAPTER 4

THE NAME OF THE FATHER, SON, AND HOLY SPIRIT

It is time to combine all that we have said thus far and to form a few brief statements summarizing the Bible's teaching of the Trinity. We will give a definition of what the Bible says the Trinity is and offer a summary of how the triune God achieves his purposes.

Definition

The definition can be arranged in three statements:

1. There is only one true God. The Bible assumes this fact throughout all that it says. For example, if there were more than one God, the Bible would not condemn the worship of many gods, which was so prevalent when the Bible was written. The Bible also states explicitly that there is only one true God. For example, Romans 3:30 says that "there is only one God, who will justify"; this means that only one God will save sinners. Galatians 3:20 includes the statement that "God is one." First Timothy 1:17 praises God as "the King eternal, immortal, invisible, the only God." James teaches that even the demons know this about God. It says, "You believe that there is one God. Good! Even the demons believe that—and shudder" (James 2:19). Deuteronomy teaches that this truth means we should devote ourselves to this one true God. "Hear, O Israel: The LORD our God, the LORD is one. Love the LORD your God with all your heart and with all your soul and with all your strength" (Deuteronomy 6:4–5). A foundational biblical truth is that there is only one true God.

2. This one true God exists as three distinct persons. Just as it is difficult to define what a human person is, so it is difficult to define a divine person. However, in human relationships different persons are distinct, with unique qualities, yet they can relate to each other in a "personal" way. The same is true of the divine persons in a far more exalted sense. They are distinct, but they relate to each other personally. For example, we have seen in chapter 2 how the Bible teaches that the Father is distinct from the Son and that the Father sent the Son. We have also shown from the Bible in chapter 3 that the Holy Spirit is a divine person who deals with Jesus' disciples in a personal way by teaching, reminding, and guiding them. Although one God, the Father, Son, and Holy Spirit are distinct persons.

Jesus employed these first two statements of our definition when he sent his disciples into the world to preach the gospel. He told his apostles to "make disciples of all nations, baptizing them in the name of the Father and of the Son and of the Holy Spirit" (Matthew 28:19). Jesus did not say that the nations must be baptized in the "names," as though there were many names and many gods. He says "name," meaning one. But when the one "name" is given, Jesus mentions three: Father, Son, and Holy Spirit. The one true God exists as three distinct persons.

3. Each person is fully divine. This has been shown in chapters 1 and 3. As we have seen, the Bible calls each person—Father, Son, and Holy Spirit—"God." We noticed this in Colossians 2:9, which says that "in Christ all the fullness of the Deity lives in bodily form." We also noticed that in Acts 5:4 Peter calls the Holy Spirit "God." This truth about the Holy Spirit is confirmed in 1 Corinthians 3:16–17, where we learn both that the Christian is God's temple, which means the house of God, and that God's Spirit lives in the Christian believer. According to these verses God's house is where the Spirit lives; the Spirit is God. These verses are calling the Father, Son, and Holy Spirit "God."

This third statement in our definition, however, does not mean there are three gods. As the first statement shows, the Bible says there is only one true God.

Summary

We have also learned in these chapters how the triune God achieves his purposes. We can summarize by saying, "The Father works of himself, *through the* Son, *in the*

Spirit" (Herman Bavinck, *The Doctrine of God*, trans. William Hendriksen [Grand Rapids: Baker, 1977], 318). Or we can say that the Father does all things through the Son by the power of the Holy Spirit.

We have seen that the Father *created* all things through the Son (John 1:3; 1 Corinthians 8:6; Colossians 1:16) by the Spirit's power (Genesis 1:2; Psalm 104:30). We have also seen that God the Father *saved* his people by sending his Son in the Spirit's power.

We cannot comprehend all this, yet this incomprehensible and amazing God has made clear to us how we can know him. We need not settle for vague notions concerning what God might be like, nor should we craft ideas about God that come from our own minds or from currently popular opinions. God the Father came to us through God the Son by God the Spirit's power; this is how he has shown himself to us.

So men and women of all races in all ages must come near to God the Father using the same path of approach: through Jesus Christ. We must turn away from our sins, confessing to God that what the Bible says about our sinful hearts and our sinful deeds is true. We must confess to God that we are unable to save ourselves from his judgment on our sins. Then we must entrust ourselves completely for all eternity to Jesus Christ, who died to remove our sins. We must believe that Jesus' death and resurrection were sufficient payment for all our sins. We must trust that, by resting in him, we have Christ as our shelter from God's coming judgment. We must understand that Jesus Christ was qualified to save us because he was sent by his heavenly Father and empowered by the Holy Spirit to accomplish this salvation. The Father and Spirit direct our faith to what God did in Jesus.

Then, we must continue to live out this trust in Christ, following what his Word, the Bible, commands and resting continually in the certainty of the salvation he has given. Our endeavors to know God must send us to Christ throughout all our lives. After we have entrusted ourselves to Jesus Christ, we must understand that the Holy Spirit gave us the desire to do so.

God the Father offers eternal salvation from our sins through his gift Jesus Christ, who came by the Spirit's power. Let us each approach the Father using the same pathway. As the Bible says, through Christ "we . . . have access to the Father by one Spirit" (Ephesians 2:18).

Questions

For Review
1. State and explain each of the three parts of the definition of the Trinity.
2. How do the persons of the Trinity work together as one God?

For Further Thought
3. How do the following verses support our definition of the Trinity?
   a. John 6:44
   b. 1 John 4:2
   c. John 8:58 compared with Exodus 3:14
4. How do the following verses support our summary of the work of the Trinity?
   a. Luke 1:34–35
   b. 2 Corinthians 5:18
5. What must you do to be saved from your sins?

CHAPTER 5

BECAUSE OF HIS MERCY

We have seen that throughout the Bible God shows himself to be triune, one God existing as three distinct persons. It may be helpful now for us to examine several places in the Bible where the three persons of the Trinity are mentioned side by side. Doing so will confirm for us the truth that each of the three persons is distinct yet works with the other two in all things concerning the Christian's salvation.

The portions of the Bible that we will examine teach us that Christians receive God's mercy. Therefore, these biblical passages that confirm our understanding of the Trinity will also teach us how the salvation that a Christian experiences comes from the three persons of the Trinity working as one.

Titus 3:4–7

The book of the Bible that we call "Titus" was written by the apostle Paul to a man named Titus, a church pastor or elder who served Christ on the island of Crete. In these verses Paul directs Titus to teach the Christians of Crete to devote themselves to doing what is good (Titus 3:8). As Titus teaches Christians to do what is good, he reminds them what they once were like and what the triune God has done for them.

In the past they were characterized by ongoing sin. Not only were they guilty of actively disobeying God and hating one another, but they also were characterized by a sinful temperament. Furthermore, they were enslaved to sin. "At one time we too were foolish, disobedient, deceived and enslaved by all kinds of passions and pleasures. We lived in malice and envy, being hated and hating one another" (Titus 3:3). They practiced sin, were characterized by sin, and were enchained by sin. They were guilty, rebellious, and spiritually powerless. This describes the essential problem of all people who do not believe in Jesus Christ for salvation from sin. Sin characterizes their heart. The Bible says, "The heart is deceitful above all things and beyond cure" (Jeremiah 17:9).

But "God our Savior" showed mercy (Titus 3:4). We discover, as we read these verses, that "God our Savior" refers to God the Father. He is the one who poured out the Holy Spirit and did that generously through Jesus Christ our Savior (Titus 3:6). When God the Father saved his people, he (in the words of one Christian hymn) saved them from sin's guilt and power. This means God the Father provided a way for the guilty record of sinners to be erased and the enslaving power of sin to be destroyed. To show mercy, he sent Jesus Christ, and he poured out the Holy Spirit.

The fact that God saves from the power of sin can be seen in the saving work of the Holy Spirit. God saved us "through the washing of rebirth and renewal by the Holy Spirit" (Titus 3:5). Instead of saying that we were enslaved by sin, this verse adds to that truth by implying that we were dead in sin. So God the Holy Spirit, because of his mercy, gave new life to the sinner so that he could believe in Christ. He washed that sinner's heart, which was contaminated by sin. The Spirit performed this miracle of grace in the Christian's heart. The sinner didn't renovate himself and give himself a new life. Rather, the Holy Spirit brought about this rebirth and renewal. Because of the Holy Spirit, the sinner's heart and life were changed.

But God also saves from sin's guilt. The Spirit was "poured out . . . generously through Jesus Christ our Savior" (Titus 3:6). Since the Holy Spirit is the Spirit of Christ, his merciful gift of rebirth and renewal is connected to what "Jesus Christ our Savior" did. The Lord Jesus died on the cross to suffer the punishment sinners deserve. He took their place. All those who place their faith in Jesus Christ are, therefore, justified. Justification is the jury's decision concerning someone who is accused. If the jury declares a man to be innocent, that man is justified. God justifies sinners. He declares them not guilty, and those who receive his justification by faith in Christ will never face God's eternal punishment. They are freed from God's eternal justice because, on the cross, Christ endured God's justice in their place. In God's eyes their guilt is gone.

Although members of Titus's church had been guilty of sin and were enslaved to sin, they received justification through faith in Christ and renewal of their hearts by the Holy Spirit. The result was that they possessed the confident hope of eternal life. All this was given to them because of the mercy of the triune God.

Ephesians 1:3–14

In this introductory section of his letter to Christians living in Ephesus the apostle Paul praises the triune God for his amazing grace. God the Father has "blessed us in the heavenly realms with every spiritual blessing" (Ephesians 1:3). But it becomes clear that the Father was not alone when he saved the church. "Every spiritual blessing" was given "in Christ."

Paul proceeds to teach about God's ways, which no human mind can comprehend. The Father chose those whom he would save. He chose them before the world began with the purpose that they should be "holy and blameless in his sight" and become adopted children of God (Ephesians 1:4–5).

All that the Father planned for them he planned to bring about through Jesus Christ. "He predestined us to be adopted as his sons through Jesus Christ" (Ephesians 1:5). Jesus made this adoption possible through his death on the cross. By his death on the cross he bought them back (achieved "redemption") and granted the forgiveness of sins (Ephesians 1:7). In this way Christ carried out the plan of the Father for those whom the Father chose. The Father saved them through Christ, the Son.

But there is more. The Christians in Ephesus received God's gift of adoption through Christ when they heard "the gospel of your salvation" (Ephesians 1:13), and this was possible because of the gift of the Holy Spirit. The Holy Spirit is God's deposit in the heart of the Christian (Ephesians 1:14).

When Jesus returns, he will give the Christian every part of heavenly glory that he planned and promised. But, for now, the Christian has received God's down payment of that final glory; he has been given the Holy Spirit. When a home buyer pays 10 percent down, he is committing himself to pay the rest—either with money he already has or with money he will borrow. Similarly, by giving the follower of Christ the Holy Spirit, God the Father has committed himself to giving the Christian the rest of heavenly glory.

We can see from Ephesians 1 how the triune God has saved us. The Father planned to show his mercy; the Son carried out on the cross what was necessary for mercy to be given; the Holy Spirit's power enables Christians to receive that mercy by faith in Jesus Christ. As the Bible says, "For it is by grace you have been saved, through faith—and this not from yourselves, it is the gift of God—not by works, so that no one can boast" (Ephesians 2:8–9).

Other Scriptures

Let us note briefly where the three persons of the Trinity appear together in other places of the Bible. For example, when Jesus was baptized, the Spirit of God descended on him like a dove. Also, a voice from heaven, the voice of God the Father, said of Jesus, "This is my Son, whom I love; with him I am well pleased" (Matthew 3:16–17). The three persons participated, therefore, at the beginning of Jesus' public ministry.

In another place, Ephesians 4 teaches that the church of Christ is one. It does so with many proofs, including the fact that there is only one Father, one Son, and one Holy Spirit. "There is one body and one Spirit . . . one Lord [Jesus], one faith, one baptism; one God and Father of all, who is over all and through all and in all" (Ephesians 4:4–6). Since one Father, one Son, and one Spirit saved the church, this proves the unity of the true church.

In yet another instance, Paul pronounces God's blessing on the church by referring to the three persons of the triune God: "May the grace of the Lord Jesus Christ, and the love of God [the Father], and the fellowship of the Holy Spirit be with you all" (2 Corinthians 13:14).

And, as we have noticed before, Jesus commanded the church to baptize in the name of the triune God: "Therefore go and make disciples of all nations, baptizing them in the name of the Father and of the Son and of the Holy Spirit" (Matthew 28:19). God wants this triune name—announcing God's ownership—placed on those who follow Christ. They are all disciples because of God's mercy, mercy from Father, Son, and Holy Spirit.

In each instance we can see how the Bible regards the Father, Son, and Holy Spirit as distinct persons. But we also notice that they as one God have acted together to present us with a deliverance from sin that is complete and fully desirable to those who understand their sinfulness before God. The Father sent Christ, and the Spirit empowered Jesus Christ to accomplish escape from sin's guilt and power for all those who turn to Jesus for mercy.

Questions

For Review
1. According to Titus 3:4–7, how did each person of the Trinity show mercy?
2. According to Ephesians 1:3–14, what did each person of the Trinity do to save God's people?

For Further Thought

3. How do the following verses suggest the presence of the Trinity?
   a. Genesis 1:26
   b. Genesis 3:22
   c. Genesis 11:7
   d. Isaiah 6:8

CHAPTER 6

TO SEE IF IT
IS TRUE

During one of the apostle Paul's journeys, while he preached the way of salvation through Christ, his hearers in the city of Berea responded in a unique way. Whereas in some places those who heard Paul quickly reacted strongly against his teaching, the people in Berea "were of more noble character." They "examined the Scriptures every day to see if what Paul said was true" (Acts 17:11).

Perhaps you have read this book with interest but still have questions that must be answered. You may still want to see if what you have read here is true.

Throughout the history of the Christian church many challenges have been raised against the Bible's teaching concerning the Trinity. Often these challenges have focused on who Jesus Christ was and is. There have been so many different objections against the teaching of the Trinity—and each objection has been expressed in so many ways—that it is impossible to list and answer them all. The challenges tend to fall, however, into a few groups. The objections we cover here represent most of those groups.

What follows is both a summary of the teaching concerning the Trinity and Jesus Christ and answers to objections concerning the Bible's teaching. My hope is that this process will answer the questions still on your mind, and you will discover that what you have read here is true.

I should add that, although the church in its councils throughout history summarized the Bible's teaching using very specific terminology, I am attempting here to convey the meaning of biblical teaching with everyday words.

The Trinity

Summary of the Bible's Teaching Concerning the Trinity

- There is only one true God.
- He exists as three distinct persons.
- Each person is fully divine.

Objections Concerning the Trinity

1. The Trinity is not a logical idea. How can you believe it?

It is true that when God created man good, God gave mankind the ability to reason and think through issues. However that does not mean that human reason or logic is without limitations. In fact, there are places in the Bible where God disagrees with the logical conclusions that people reach. For example, the book of Romans expresses questions that people might logically ask based on the apostle Paul's teaching. In various places in his letters Paul introduces such logical questions with, "What shall we say, then?" Such questions are followed with God's response: "By no means!" (Romans 6:2, 15) and "Who are you, O man, to talk back to God?" (Romans 9:20). Human reason is neither flawless nor comprehensive.

It must also be said that God is far greater than the human mind's reason or comprehension. In the Bible God says,

> "My thoughts are not your thoughts,
>   neither are your ways my ways," declares the LORD.
> "As the heavens are higher than the earth,
>   so are my ways higher than your ways
>   and my thoughts than your thoughts."
>   (Isaiah 55:8–9)

God's Word also says that God "is able to do immeasurably more than all we ask or imagine" (Ephesians 3:20).

Therefore, when we refer to the triune God, we are describing a God who is greater than our logic and minds. We believe the teaching of the Trinity because this is what eternal God has taught us about himself. We believe it because God said it, not because we understand it or because we can logically explain it.

2. If Father, Son, and Holy Spirit are all divine, why don't we say there are three Gods?

The view that there are three Gods, sometimes called "tritheism," has not been widely held among those who claim to follow the Bible (although Mormonism claims there are many gods). This view, that there are three Gods, tries to apply logic to the truth that Father, Son, and Holy Spirit are all God.

This teaching denies that part of our definition of the Trinity which says that there is only one God. The Bible, however, makes clear that there is only one God and that God is one (Deuteronomy 6:4; Isaiah 40:25).

3. If there is only one God, shouldn't we understand the Father, Son, and Holy Spirit to be different expressions of the same person (i.e., one person with three costumes)?

Sometimes the view that God is one divine person who has displayed himself in three different ways is based on analogies from nature to show that this is a logical way to think of God (for example, water exists in three different modes: ice, liquid, and steam). Sometimes this view maintains that God adopted these different modes of existence at different times in biblical history—first as Creator and lawgiver (Father), then as Redeemer (Son), and finally as giver of grace (Holy Spirit). This view, in all its varieties, denies that the persons of God are distinct; it denies, for example, that the Father is distinct in person from the Son.

We have seen especially in chapters 2 and 3 how the Bible teaches that there are three distinct persons. The Father is the Father *of* our Lord Jesus Christ (Ephesians 1:3) and is the one who sent the Son (John 16:5). The Father and the Son sent the Holy Spirit (John 14:26; 15:26); they did not send themselves. When we notice in the Bible how these three persons interact with each other, we conclude that, although they exist as one God, they are distinct persons.

4. If there is only one God, wouldn't it be better to say that only the Father is the one supreme God, and that the Son and the Holy Spirit are lesser beings or powers?

This view so stresses the unity of God that it denies that

all of the three persons are fully divine. Its many adherents hold to a great variety of opinions concerning how to explain the unity of God. Jehovah's Witnesses, for example, believe that only the Father is God, that the Son is the Father's first creature and may be considered a lesser god, and that the Holy Spirit is neither personal nor divine. A different viewpoint, that of New Age followers (to the extent that they use biblical terminology), maintains that one God is in everything, including Jesus Christ.

These views do not take into account all of the Bible's teaching concerning the Son and the Holy Spirit. Both, along with the Father, are called "God" in the Bible (Colossians 2:9; Acts 5:4; 1 Corinthians 3:16–17). Both, the Son and Holy Spirit, along with the Father, were fully involved in doing what only God did: they created the universe (Genesis 1:1; John 1:3; Psalm 104:30) and saved sinners (Luke 1:47; Titus 1:4). These views also disregard the equal standing Jesus gave to all three persons in Matthew 28:19.

Although this challenge seeks to preserve the unity of God, which the Bible also does, it does so in a way that contradicts the Bible's teaching concerning the divinity of the Son and Holy Spirit.

Jesus Christ

Summary of the Bible's Teaching Concerning Jesus Christ

- From eternity the Son of God has been divine in person and nature.
- When he was conceived of the virgin Mary by the Holy Spirit's power, he added to himself our human nature.

- Since then and for all eternity to come, he remains one divine person possessing two distinct natures; one is divine and the other is human.

Objections Concerning Jesus Christ

5. Doesn't the Bible teach in the following ways that Jesus is not divine but is inferior to the Father?

Jesus prayed to his Father. The fact that the eternal Son of God added to himself our human nature is indeed a mystery beyond our comprehension. Since this is so, some aspects of Jesus' life on earth reflect the fact that he was God, and other aspects indicate that he was man. The fact that he prayed showed him to be a man.

Nevertheless, Jesus' prayers did not all indicate that he was only a man. In one of his prayers Jesus said, "And now, Father, glorify me in your presence with the glory I had with you before the world began" (John 17:5). Even when Jesus prayed, he referred to the divine glory that belonged eternally to him and the Father together.

Jesus referred to "my God." One place where Jesus refers to his Father as "my God" is John 20:17. In that verse Jesus explains immediately after his resurrection that he had not yet returned to his Father. But, Jesus said, "I am returning to my Father and your Father, to my God and your God" (John 20:17).

One thing we notice is that Jesus did not say *"our* Father" and *"our* God." This, in itself, hints that Jesus is God. Jesus is divine, and we are not. Therefore, while Jesus' relationship to his Father is similar to ours, his relationship with God is unique. He is God's *eternal* son. Yet, because he died for his followers, Christians enjoy a privilege that is most similar to his (D. A. Carson, *The Gospel According to John* [Grand Rapids: Eerdmans, 1991], 645). They are now *adopted* children of God (Romans 8:15–16) and therefore they are Jesus' brothers (Hebrews 2:11–12).

We can say more. The fact that Jesus calls his Father "my God" does not have to mean that Jesus is less than God. It only teaches that he submitted to God the Father's will. The relationship between the Father and the Son is similar to the relationship between Moses and Aaron in Exodus 4:16. There God says that Moses will be given God's Word. Moses must teach it to Aaron so that Aaron can tell the people. God said to Moses, Aaron "will speak to the people for you, and it will be as if he were your mouth and as if you were God to him." Moses was not "God to him" because he was a greater being, but because he was given the authority of God's Word. Similarly, the Father is the God of Jesus because Jesus submitted himself to the Father's will.

Jesus said, "the Father is greater than I." Jesus said this in John 14:28, where he refers to the fact that he will return to the Father. When he came, Jesus submitted to his Father's will. He said, "I do exactly what my Father has commanded" (John 14:31). The Father was greater because Jesus lived under his Father's authority. However, we should never forget what Jesus also said in John 10:30: "I and the Father are one."

Jesus is called "the firstborn over all creation." This title for Jesus can be found in Colossians 1:15. Some say that this designation teaches that Jesus was the first creature that the Father made. But this is a misunderstanding of the term "firstborn."

"Firstborn" refers to the status usually given to the first-born son, though not always. In ancient times the firstborn son ranked highest in the family after the father. He also received an inheritance twice as great as the inheritance of his brothers (Deuteronomy 21:15–17).

However, 1 Chronicles 5:2 shows that in Israel's family the rights of the firstborn were given to Joseph. Joseph was not born first. Rather, in the series of twelve sons born to his father Jacob, Joseph was born eleventh. Nevertheless, due to a series of events that we will not review here, Joseph was given the honor and authority of the firstborn.

When the Bible calls Jesus "the firstborn over all creation," it does not imply that Jesus was created first. Rather, it teaches that he possessed honor and authority over the creation. That is precisely what the following verse also teaches: "All things were created by him and for him" (Colossians 1:16).

The Bible says, "The head of Christ is God." This statement is found in 1 Corinthians 11:3. Just before it is this statement: "The head of the woman is man." This statement concerning the man and woman does not teach that the man is a being superior to the woman. Therefore, we should not conclude that this verse teaches that God the Father is a being superior to Christ. This verse is describing people under authority. The wife is under the husband's authority just as Christ is under God the Father's authority.

Jesus was called the Son of God. In human relationships a son does not possess a humanity that is inferior to his father's. Similarly, the Son's divinity is not inferior to God the Father's. As we mentioned in chapter 1, when Jesus called himself the Son of God, he was understood to mean that he was equal with God (John 5:18). Instead of changing this understanding of what he said, Jesus was willing to be persecuted and eventually crucified because of what the title "Son of God" meant for him: that he was equal with God.

Although this list does not exhaust all the ways the Bible is used to deny the full divinity of Jesus Christ, these answers can be used as a guide concerning how other questions about the Bible's teaching should be answered.

6. Shouldn't we say Jesus was a man but that God's wisdom rested on him in an extraordinary way?

This challenge, first raised many centuries ago, tries to find a way to explain how the Bible can refer to Jesus as God while maintaining that, in fact, Jesus is only human. This challenge holds the view of the Trinity that is expressed in question 4.

It denies the Bible's teaching that Jesus was in the beginning with the Father (John 1:1–2) and that Jesus was God even before Abraham (John 8:58). But these verses of the Bible teach that Jesus is God eternally.

7. Isn't it possible that Jesus was God and he only appeared to be a man?

This challenge denies the real humanity of Jesus Christ and rejects what the Bible says about Jesus' humanity. The gospel of John says, "The Word became flesh" (John 1:14). Peter said, "Jesus of Nazareth was a man" (Acts 2:22). First John 4:2 says, "This is how you can recognize the Spirit of

God: Every spirit that acknowledges that Jesus Christ has come in the flesh is from God."

8. If Jesus was both God and man, wouldn't it be best to say that he was a combination of two completely different persons, a divine person and nature and a human person and nature?

This challenge denies that the divine and human natures of Jesus Christ are united in any real way.

This view contradicts the Bible, which teaches that the one divine person — Jesus Christ — possesses both full divinity and full humanity. For example, John 1 says both that the "Word was God" and that "the Word became flesh" (John 1:1, 14). Isaiah 9:6 says that the name of the son to be born is "Mighty God."

9. Instead of saying that Jesus had two natures, shouldn't we say that somehow his human and divine natures were merged together and became something in between (like the alloy bronze, which, although composed of copper and tin, possesses its own unique qualities)?

This view seeks to preserve the unity of Christ by saying that, despite his being born of the virgin Mary, he remained one person with one nature. But this view denies that Jesus had the same human nature that we have since, according to this view, it was merged with Jesus' divinity.

The Bible corrects this view by saying that Jesus possessed a human nature just like ours except only for sin (Hebrews 2:17; 4:15). This similarity of Jesus to us is vital to our salvation. Since Jesus possessed our human nature, he was able to take the place of human sinners.

CONCLUSION

This book has attempted to present as clearly as possible the Trinity—the God who saves. The triune God has made available to us his mercy in a way that is based on what he is like. He is one God who exists as three distinct persons. Nevertheless, although distinct, these three persons work together in infinite community. In the light of our sin and God's just punishment of sin, the Father sent the Son by the power of the Holy Spirit.

Consider, for a moment, the complete adequacy of this divine Savior Jesus. As the Son of God, he came in the Spirit's power, which prepared him perfectly to be our Savior, and he has completely fulfilled the requirements the Father laid down for our sins to be totally forgiven. As God, he is able to stand before his holy Father to offer his complete and acceptable sacrifice for sin. As man, he was close enough to us to take our place. The book of Hebrews teaches these qualifications of Jesus by saying that Christ "entered heaven itself, now to appear for us in God's presence" (Hebrews 9:24). There is no one else able or qualified to save us from our sins.

This is the Savior God offers to us so that we can find forgiveness. He commands us to trust in this Jesus Christ, repenting of our sins and trusting that Jesus has paid for all our sins. He tells us in the Bible that once we have turned to Christ for forgiveness, we must continue to follow him by obeying his Word and relying on the power of his Spirit. If we are trusting in Christ, he has promised that at the end of this phase of history he will return visibly to take us to be with him forever. Then as God's children we will see and enjoy the privileges that Christ earned for his followers.

Have you ever been offered a more wonderful salvation—from such a perfect Savior? Study the verses in the Bible that this book has repeatedly cited and see for yourself whether the triune God's offer of salvation in Jesus Christ is true.

SUGGESTED READING

Works Specifically Concerning the Trinity

Erickson, Millard J. *Making Sense of the Trinity: Three Crucial Questions.* Grand Rapids: Baker, 2000.

Olyott, Stuart. *The Three Are One.* Durham, England: Evangelical Press, 1979.

Payne, Robert. "A Hammer Struck at Heresy." *Christian History* 15 (July/August 1996): 11–19.

White, James. *The Forgotten Trinity.* Minneapolis: Bethany House, 1998.

Works Containing a Chapter on the Trinity

Berkhof, L. *Systematic Theology.* 4th ed. Grand Rapids: Eerdmans, 1941.

Boice, James Montgomery. *Foundations of the Christian Faith.* Rev. ed. Downers Grove: InterVarsity, 1986.

Reymond, Robert L. *A New Systematic Theology of the Christian Faith.* Nashville: Nelson, 1998.

INDEX OF SCRIPTURE